"When the door of happiness closes,
another opens, but often we look so long
at the closed door that we do not see the one
which has been opened for us."
Helen Keller

For Lorraine Jolian Cazin
who encouraged me to trust myself

# Fly With Me

A Fusion of Images and Poetry
by Ute Buehler

Fly with Me
A Fusion of Images and Poetry by Ute Buehler

Copyright © 2012 Ute Buehler
Photography, Layout and Design by Ute Buehler
www.buehlers.net
First printed 2012

ISBN 10: 0-9770749-2-1
ISBN 13: 978-0-9770749-2-1

Published in the United States by
Studio 214 Publishing
501 Main Street North, Ste 214
Stillwater, Minnesota 55082 - U.S.A.
www.Studio214Publishing.net

Printed in the United States
www.lightningsource.com

# Foreword

*Fly With Me* is Ute Buehler's first book of poetry. While German is her native language, she shows a mastery of English, and the artistry of poetry and photography in this book. Each poem and each photograph is beautifully integrated. Together they set forth her vision of art, creativity, and a broad understanding of the nature of love.

The book's title, *Fly With Me*, which comes from a poem by that name, aptly describes the sanguinity in her poetry. In the poem itself, Ute offers a myriad of viewpoints on the significance of a feather. The poem's final line is an unexpected invitation to fly away with her to the other realms that she portrays in both her photography and words.

One of those realms is the world of creativity. In the poem, "The Ripple, the Bubble and the Burst," she describes the birth of an idea that results in the compulsion that all artists feel—that eruption of a need to write, to paint, to take a picture—to share the insight that has come to them. She speaks to the artist in all of us that says I must write, I must paint, I must create, if I am to live. In her poem, "The Poet," she describes the lack of confidence that so many artists and writers feel.

She acknowledges all those whose inspiration and support gave her the courage to try. Finally, she expresses the joy that comes with the realization that she is, in fact, a poet.

Another realm Ute explores is the world of love. " The Giver," "Fences," and "My Child," give us intimate glimpses into how her family, friends and children have enriched her life. The poem, "Spring Serenade," teaches us that attraction is not dependent on beauty, and "This Day Gone By" shows us its endurance.

In *Fly With Me,* it is hard to know what came first, the poems or the pictures because what they all do is create a sense of optimism. These poems are filled with honesty and hopefulness, even when dealing with weighty subjects such as a diagnosis of cancer.

Ute shares a sensibility of buoyancy and beauty that enriches us. I look forward to more of her writing and photography.

Kathleen Pettit, Poet
Director, Bloomington Writers' Festival

## The Poems and Their Photographs

## The Ripple, the Bubble and the Burst

Ideas are forming deep within ...
there is a ripple in my ocean,
wider it grows, its circles rising to the surface

First little bubbles pop up in the air,
bigger and yet bigger bubbles
gurgling with delight

More and bigger spurts of bubbles spring up
from the surface of this ocean,
like a volcano close to its eruption

The waters burst,
the thoughts shoot out like geysers,
erupting from within the vision

And high above the ocean this fountain springs,
high up into the air to catch the sunlight,
to be nourished by the warmth

To fall down again as showers,
back into the ocean ...
to be transformed

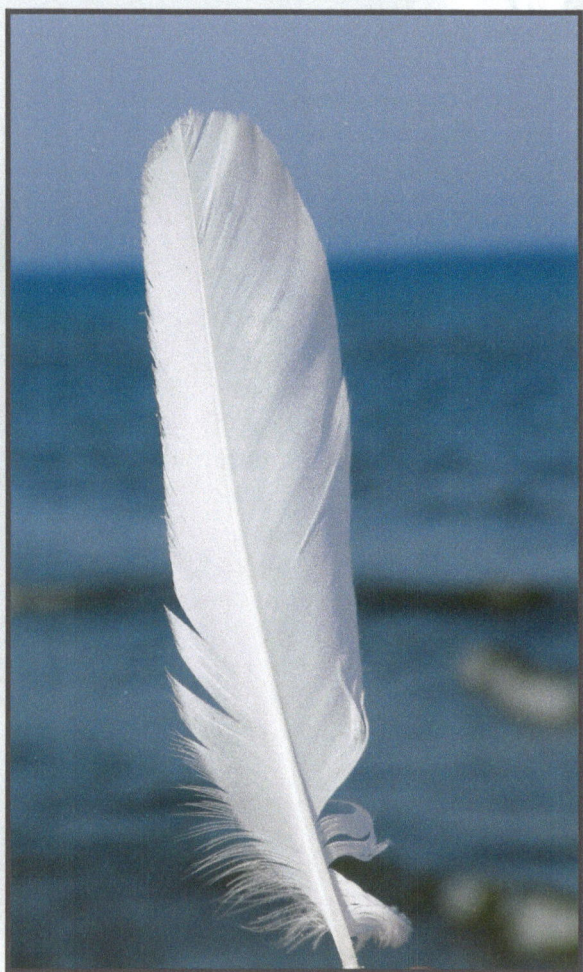

## Fly With Me

I found a feather on the beach today.

They say
"Feathers tell of honor and brave deeds"

He says
"Feathers carry birds to distant shores"

She says
"Feathers make the eagle soar"

They say
"Feathers render wings to our souls"

She says
"Feathers must be given to a friend"

I say
"Take this feather, friend, come,
        fly with me"

## Spring Serenade

The blackbird's swinging on a reed,
weightlessly,
swaying gently in the breeze

I watch it spreading out its wings
and opening its beak and, no, not singing out,
but croaking out its song

No, to my ears there is no beauty in its voice,
yet it is sending out a serenade
to call a lover

I hold this memory as a reminder, that,
no matter how we croak
or off the tune are our songs

The springtime serenade of
        "I love you"
will always be perceived as beautiful,
when listened to with our hearts

## Sip of Cappuccino

On a sunny afternoon
at the river promenade

We sit and watch,
our cups of cappuccino
resting at our elbows

Girls walk by giggling;
they share their secrets
hidden behind cupped hands

Young women saunter by;
seductively they flaunt their bodies,
shrouding their eyes behind dark glasses

We wiser women
know the joy of sharing silence—
the liberty of middle age

With relish savoring
the creamy froth of our cappuccinos
we watch with glee this bright parade of vanities—

Exchanging glances and a wink

## The Giver

She is a giver
not a taker

She gives her love
She gives her care

She gives compassion
She gives comfort

She gives advice
She gives a smile

A smile so like  this flower
filled with sunlight

A smile that links her heart to mine,
and through the windows of her eyes
            embraces me

She never seeks to take, yet,
she deserves so much

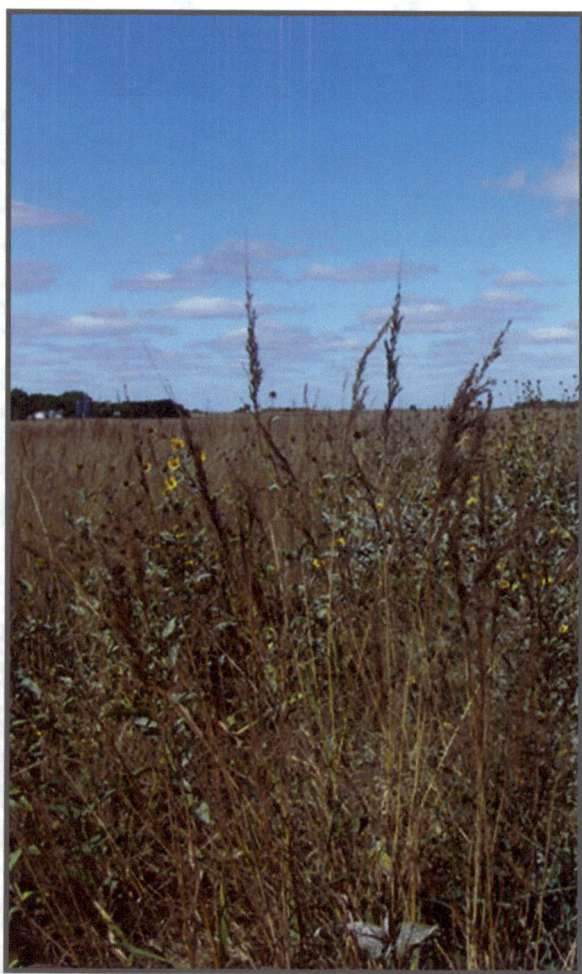

## Silence

I close my eyes; here in the prairie
the air around me vibrates
with the humming harmony of sounds

The space above is whispering
with melodies of winds
and countless insects singing out their joy

And swaying gracefully,
the grasses bend their heads
to tunes of silence

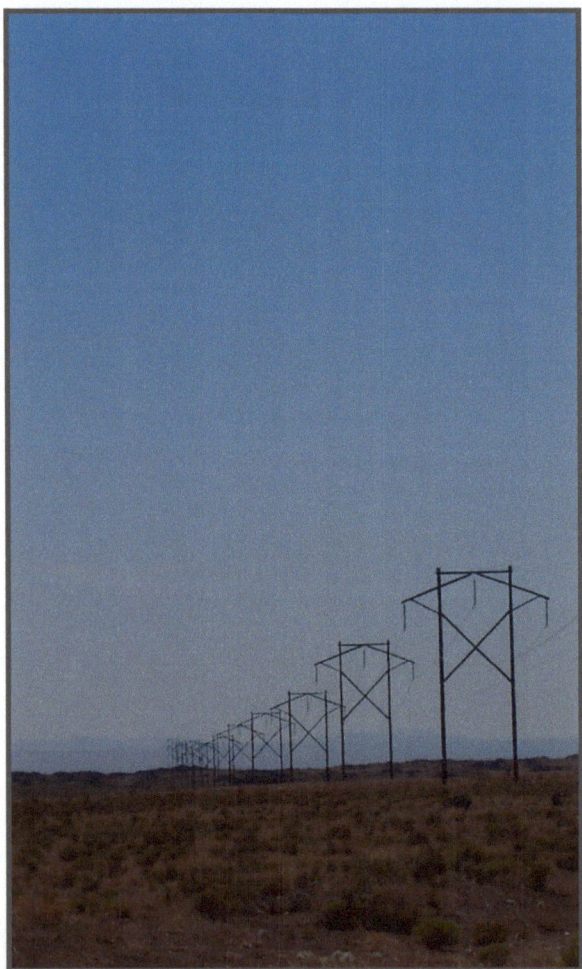

## No Fear

She woke up with a start the morning after
Surprised she should have slept at all
So—cancer it is, it is cancer
Oh my dear God—not cancer, no!

Reality is overwhelming her
Like giant waves of a tsunami
Cancer!—
And with it comes a wave of fear

This fear is what she fears
This fear that liquifies
Her limbs, her bones, her flesh
This fear that numbs her mind into a stupor

She once had read this in a book
"Thou shalt not fear, fear is the little death"
And now she understands
That she must overcome the little death—her fear

She feels that she must conquer it,
                              this worst of enemies
Let fear pass over and through her
And watch it go away
Then turn around and only she remains

And then she can stand tall
And she can feel her strength
And know that she can win

## My Child

My love for you, my child,
is warm and tender,
yet it is fierce and strong

My love for you, my child,
is full of wonder; delighted with your victories,
yet wants to shield you from the world beyond

My love for you, my child,
is knowing love,
it's wary of the time to come,
when you will leave for distant shores

Now spread your wings, my child,
and fly away, though do remember:
my home and heart are always open

Come back and lick your wounds,
then fly away again
to new adventures

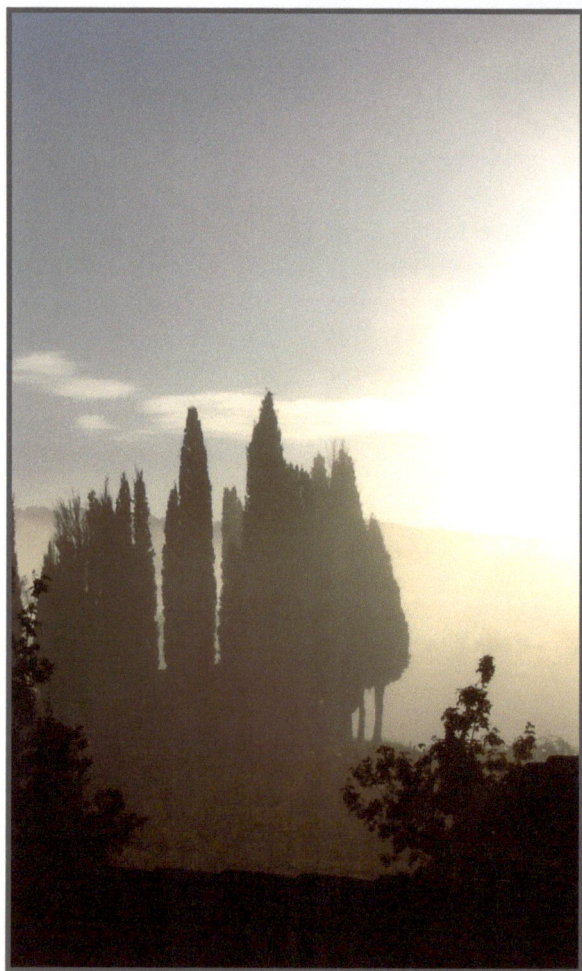

## Love

Love
this most amazing of all the emotions
selflessly giving
and yet so demanding

Love
this most challenging of all the emotions
completely trusting
and yet full of doubt

Love
this most rewarding of all the emotions
bringing bright sun to our souls
and happiness without remorse

Fences

Farmers erect fences to protect
      their cattle from the wolves

I had erected fences
      around  my injured soul
      protecting me from being hurt again

Or was it to prevent me
      from reaching out too soon
      before my soul was healed?

Fences to guard me
      until the time was right to tear them down
      and trust again—

And find you

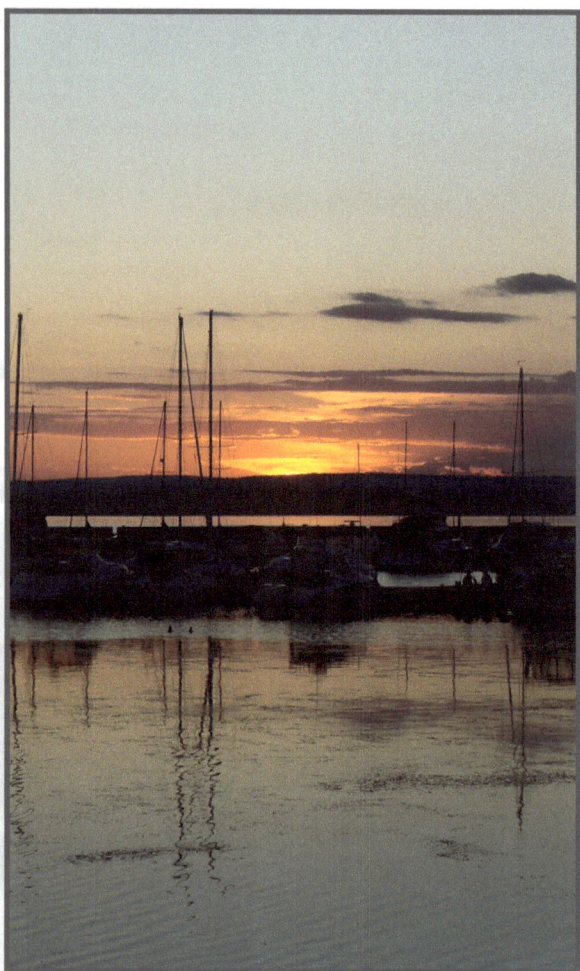

## This Day Gone By

Sunrise
We watch in awe as rays of gold
begin to shoot through purple and blue skies

We raise our arms
and breathe our yoga breath
in salutation to the rising sun

Sunset
We watch the golden streams of fading light
start turning into deepest violet and blue

We lift our faces
bidding our farewells
to one more day gone by

The hustle and the bustle
the silence and the patience
the sorrows and the joys
the wounds and the forgiveness

Another day
filled to the brim with love
A day with you

## The Poet

Words and lines keep whirling in my mind
anxiously trying to make sense,
to form the sentences,
to come out as a poem

But, I am not a poet, so how would I dare—
I could not write poems.
No, leave me alone. I am not a poet

And yet, she had said "You must try,
let go and let it happen."
And so I dare to do it, to open the gates

And now, like gushing water, the words pour out—
a flood, a river, too many, too fast, too hasty—
still, here they are

I marvel at them, join them together,
give them a melody, a rhythm.
Yes, I am doing it!

A poet I shall be

## Acknowledgments

I have dedicated this first collection of my poetry to my late fellow poet Lorraine Jolian Cazin who encouraged me to keep writing poems until she finally said "Yes, you can." Without her, this book would not exist.

My loving *thank you* to my husband for his reliable, patient and passionate support for my work, and to my friends, cheerleaders and inspirations, who gently pushed me along the path of writing.

My sincere thanks to Gail Speckmann and Connie Anderson, my editors, poets themselves, who guided me with gentle critique and great empathy, Lou Burdick and Yolanda vom Hagen for their help, and my fellow artist friends who listened, looked and critiqued with passion.

I am also grateful to the editors of *The Pen Woman Magazine (This Day Gone By)* and the *Bloomington Black Box Theater* production *Fall Fusion Poems (The Ripple, the Bubble, the Burst)* where these poems first appeared.

We say "It takes a village to raise a child," I experienced that "it takes a group of great people to give birth to a first poetry book."

Thank You.

Ute Buehler ,

## About the Poet

Born in Germany, Ute Buehler had a premonition at a very young age that her destiny would be fulfilled elsewhere in the world. This fueled a lifelong yearning to travel the world, and to record and share her perceptions.

Her creative spirit led her to photography, the perfect medium to capture her responses to the physical world as she searched Europe for "home." Ultimately, it was in North America where her spirit came to rest; her explorations there led her to expand her creative self as a photographer and writer while exploring her identity as an American citizen with passion for her new country.

Ute's photographic work has been exhibited locally and nationally, has been published internationally, and is represented in private collections; her writing is published and available online.

Home at last in the small town of Stillwater, Minnesota, Ute has discovered poetry and the freedom to explore, examine and celebrate her inner responses to life through verse.

With deep feeling and insight, Ute Buehler's words and photographic eye soar over a broad psychological landscape of family, health, and healing. Whether observing the parade of vanities along a river promenade or steeping herself and her readers in the "humming harmony of silence" on the prairie, Ute's feeling for the earth and the people who populate it is both passionate and soul-centering. In this, her first collection, Ute Buehler invites you to *Come Fly with Me*. I suggest you accept the invitation. You'll be glad you did.

> Jeanne Emrich, author of *The Pleiades at Dawn* and President of the Minnesota Branch of the National League of American Pen Women

An eye for beauty, the skill of a professional photographer, and an ability to select the precise word - the result is a "keeper."

> Peggy A. Arnett, author of The Lake Minnetonka Mysteries: *The Lady in Red - Gone But Not Forgotten*, and *Somebody Wants You Dead*

Stunning!!! The photography dances on the page and echos in shadows. Through magnificent word choice she takes us on a journey. *Fly With Me* is spiritual and thoughtful as the journey captivates us throughout. A must read.

> Linda Davis, artist and Executive Director ArtBeat, Minneapolis

www.ingramcontent.com/pod-product-compliance
Lightning Source LLC
Chambersburg PA
CBHW040749150426
42811CB00075B/1963/J